8/2013

THIS CANDLEWICK BOOK BELONGS TO:

_____

_____

_____

First U.S. paperback edition 2012

The Library of Congress has cataloged the hardcover edition as follows:

Voake, Steve.
Insect detective / Steve Voake ; illustrated by Charlotte Voake. —1st U.S. ed.
p. cm.
ISBN 978-0-7636-4447-5 (hardcover)
1. Insects—Juvenile literature. 2. Garden animals—Juvenile literature. I. Voake, Charlotte, ill. II. Title.
QL467.2.V63 2010
595.7—dc22

2009011152

ISBN 978-0-7636-5816-8
(paperback)
CCP 16 15 14 13 12 11
10 9 8 7 6 5 4 3 2 1

Printed in Shenzhen, Guangdong, China

This book was typeset
in Godlike and Charlotte.
The illustrations were done
in pen and watercolor.

Candlewick Press
99 Dover Street
Somerville, Massachusetts 02144

visit us at www.candlewick.com

CANDLEWICK PRESS

For Tory
S. V.

INSECT DETECTIVE

Steve Voake

ILLUSTRATED BY

CHARLOTTE VOAKE

RIGHT now, all around you,
thousands of insects are doing strange
and wonderful things.
But you can't always
see them right away.

Sometimes you have to know
where to look.

There
are more
insects living
in the world than all the other
animals put together—about
200 million insects for every
single person!

LISTEN—over by the fence.
Can you hear a scratching sound?
A wasp is scraping away at
the post with her strong jaws.
She's collecting wood.

She mixes it into a soft pulp
in her mouth. When she has enough,
she'll help the other wasps build
a nest out of paper.

8

Wasps
often collect
different kinds
of wood, which
makes their nests
look stripy—just
like the insects
who made
them!

Not all kinds
of wasps live together,
but many of them do.

Insects that live together are called "social insects."

Ants *always* live together.

They usually make their nests underground.

Finding an ants' nest is easy:

First find an ant . . .

then follow it.

It might stop to chat with some other

ants along the way (ants

can communicate

by touching their

antennae

together) . . .

but after a while,
the ant will head home,
and you'll be able to
find out where it lives.

Like all insects,
ants have three main
body parts.

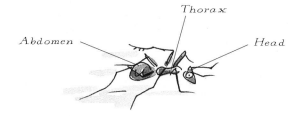

Thorax

Abdomen

Head

11

Solitary bees live by themselves (*solitary* means *alone*). This female solitary bee is busy collecting food from spring flowers. She'll store it in her tiny nest so that it will be ready for when her eggs hatch.

All insects start life as eggs.

12

Solitary bees make their
nests in holes in the ground,
cracks in walls, or in tiny
cavities that have been left
by other insects.

Many animals like to eat insects
for dinner, so some insects use camouflage
to blend in with their surroundings.

Look at this crinkly
brown leaf. Can you
see a crinkly brown
Herald moth too?

They often rest in trees during the day
so that birds won't see them.

Insects have other
ways of hiding too.
See the squiggly
lines on these leaves?
They were made by
a leaf-miner caterpillar.
The leaf miner protects
itself by living between
the top and bottom
layers of leaves—
a bit like
hiding in
a sandwich!

Lift up a stone and you might see
an earwig scuttle out. They like
to hide in the damp and the dark.
The pincers on the tips of their abdomens
make them look kind of scary,
but don't worry — they're
completely harmless.

Female earwigs are very good mothers. They work hard to keep their eggs clean, turning and washing them regularly. When the young hatch, their mothers bring them food until they're old enough to look after themselves.

Of course, you *might* find some creatures under there that aren't insects:

spiders,

centipedes,

woodlice,

slugs,

and once I found a
baby frog!

It's easy to
tell whether
something is
an insect or not.

All you have to do is count the legs:

1,   2,   3,   4,   5,   6.

If it has SIX legs, it's an insect.

If it doesn't . . . it isn't!

If you're lucky, you
might even find
a colored ground beetle gleaming in the
sunlight. It's like discovering a precious jewel!

But ground beetles aren't just pretty to look at, they're excellent hunters too. At night they go out hunting for slugs and snails, which makes gardeners very happy!

Perhaps the greatest insect hunter of all is the dragonfly. Even the name sounds fierce! But don't worry—they won't come chasing after you. Dragonflies are much more interested in catching things like flies, mosquitoes, and gnats. Some will even snatch a spider from its web.

On summer days when the air is still, you can see their wings sparkling in the light as they hunt, twisting, diving, and plucking flies from the air.

Dragonflies are fabulous fliers. They have two sets of powerful wings, which they can use to hover, change direction, and even to fly backward.

It's hard to believe they
started life in the water . . .

but dragonflies lay their eggs in ponds
or slow-moving rivers, where they hatch out
into small dragonfly "nymphs."

A nymph sheds its skin many times until
it is fully grown. Finally it climbs out of the
water and rests on the stem of a plant. As
dawn breaks, its skin splits open and a
beautiful dragonfly emerges, unfolding
its wings and drying itself in the sun.

The special changes that take place in insects' bodies
are called "metamorphoses." They happen in different
ways as insects grow from eggs to adults.

25

Sometimes, when you think about these strange and wonderful things — moths hiding, ants talking, dragonflies changing — it's hard to believe that they could really be true.

But you don't have to take my word for it.

All you have to do is open the door
and step outside.

BE AN INSECT DETECTIVE!

Find out which beetles live near you by burying a jam jar in the ground. Any beetles walking over the top during the night will fall in. But remember to check every morning and to let them go when you have finished looking.

When it gets dark, put a camping light on a white sheet outside. This will attract moths, and you will be able to get a really close look at them!

Allow a patch of nettles to grow in a corner of your yard—lots of caterpillars love to eat them. How many can you find?

Try making a place for solitary bees to live. Rinse out an empty tin can, put some glue (or melted wax) in the bottom, and fill it with drinking straws. Then hang the can with the straws pointing slightly downward to prevent rain collecting in them. When spring arrives, you'll soon see a few bees coming along to investigate!

28

Flying can
be hard work
for bumblebees.
If you see one crawling
around on the ground,
it may have run out
of energy.

Mix some sugar and water
in a teaspoon and give
the bee a drink—

it will soon be busy
among the flowers again!

Take a close look at
wooden tables, fences,
or benches you see outside.
If they have tiny lines all
over them, you'll know
a wasp has
been there
before you.

In hot,
thundery
weather, keep
an eye out
for swarming
ants. When the
temperature
is just right,
the young
queens will be
brought up to
the surface, where
they will mate
before flying
away to
start new
colonies.

INDEX

Look up the pages
to find out about
all these insect things.
Don't forget to
look at both kinds
of words—

this kind

and
this kind.

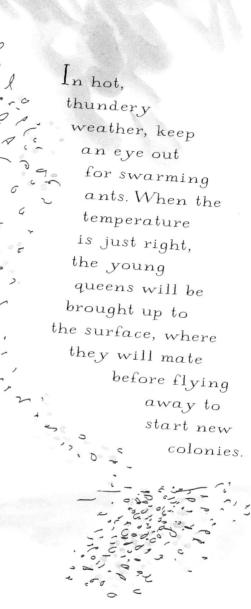

Steve Voake is the author of the Daisy Dawson series, illustrated by Jessica Meserve, and several novels for young adults. About *Insect Detective*, he says, "I've always been fascinated by insects, so when the chance came to write a book about them, illustrated by my cousin Charlotte, I couldn't wait to get started!" Steve Voake lives in England.

Charlotte Voake is the illustrator of *Caterpillar, Caterpillar*, written by Vivian French, and the author-illustrator of many award-winning picture books, including *Hello Twins*. About this book, she says, "Steve's and my grandmother had a tiny pond full of frogs, newts, and fish, and the insects loved it. She was passionate about wildlife — so perhaps we got the 'bug' from her!" Charlotte Voake lives in England.